THE PLANETARY SOCIETY

THE SUN

OUR SOLAR SYSTEM'S STAR

Bruce Betts, PhD

Lerner Publications ◆ Minneapolis

THE PLANETS AND MOONS IN OUR SOLAR SYSTEM ARE OUT OF THIS WORLD. Some are hotter than an oven, and some are much colder than a freezer. Some are small and rocky, while others are huge and mostly made of gas. As you explore these worlds, you'll discover giant canyons, active volcanoes, strange kinds of ice, storms bigger than Earth, and much more.

The Planetary Society® empowers people around the world to advance space science and exploration. On behalf of The Planetary Society®, including our tens of thousands of members, here's wishing you the joy of discovery.

Onward,

Bill Nye

Bill Nye
CEO, The Planetary Society®

Table of Contents

CHAPTER 1

OUR SOLAR SYSTEM'S STAR

The Sun is a star. A star is a huge ball of hot, glowing plasma. Stars are much hotter than fire. The Sun gives light and heat that makes life possible on Earth.

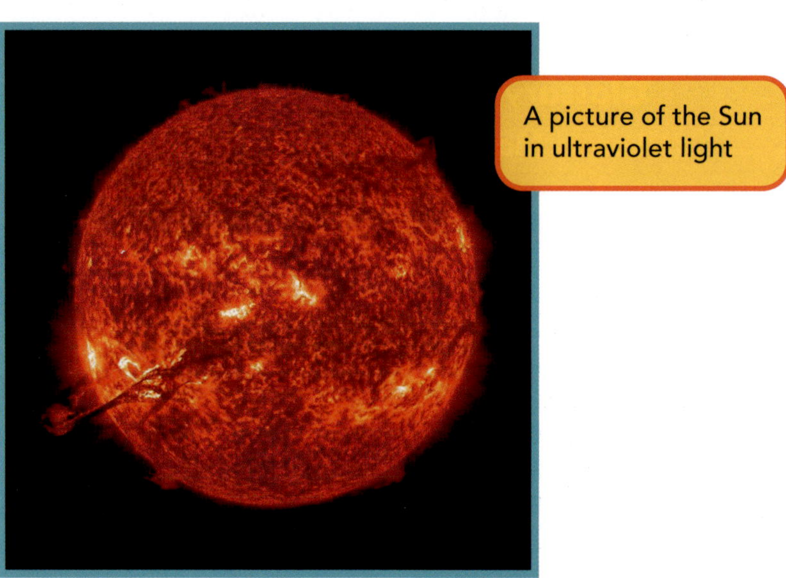

A picture of the Sun in ultraviolet light

The Sun in Space

The Sun is the center of our solar system. The word *solar* means "having to do with the Sun." So, we live in the Sun's system.

THE SUN FAST FACTS

Size	Could fit about one million Earths inside the Sun
Distance from Earth	About 93 million miles (150 million km)
Rotation period	About twenty-four to thirty Earth days to spin around once
Temperature	About 27,000,000°F (15,000,000°C) at the center

Art showing dust and gas in a newly formed planetary system

The Sun formed about five billion years ago. Gravity caused gas and dust in space to start pulling in more gas and dust. Enough gas and dust came together to form the Sun. The rest became the other objects in our solar system.

The solar system is all the objects that go around the Sun. These include planets and moons. Other stars have their own systems and planets.

The Sun is part of a group of more than one hundred million stars. Huge groups of stars are called galaxies. Our galaxy is called the Milky Way.

The Milky Way is enormous. It is 100,000 light-years across. That means it takes light one hundred thousand years to get from one side of the galaxy to the other.

The Milky Way Galaxy looks like a spiral or pinwheel.

Sun vs. Earth
If the Sun were the size of a basketball, Earth would be the size of a sesame seed.

Meet the Sun

The Sun is huge! It is much larger than the planets. More than one million Earths could fit inside the Sun.

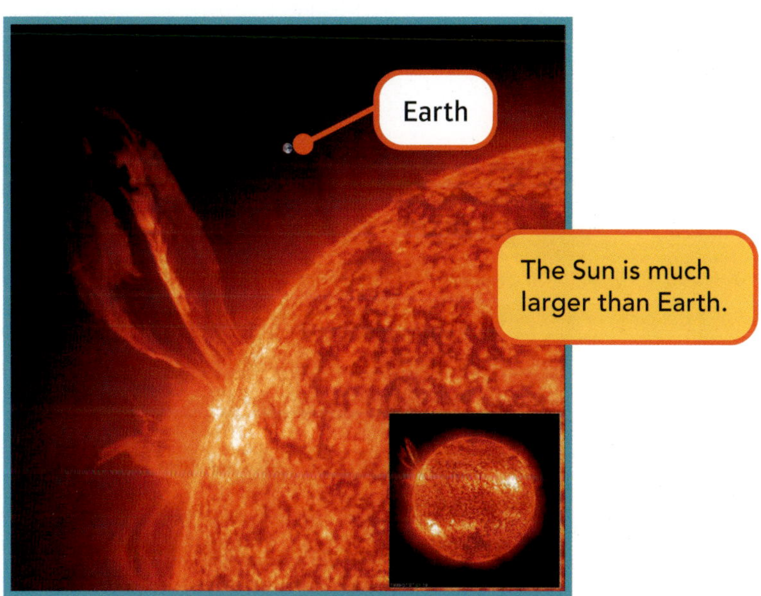

The Sun is the heaviest and largest object in the solar system. The Sun holds over 99 percent of the mass of the solar system.

Gravity is the force that holds you to the ground. Earth's gravity is also what causes objects to drop.

The more mass an object has, the stronger its pull. The Sun's gravity is so strong that all the planets and other objects in the solar system feel its pull. That keeps them from flying away.

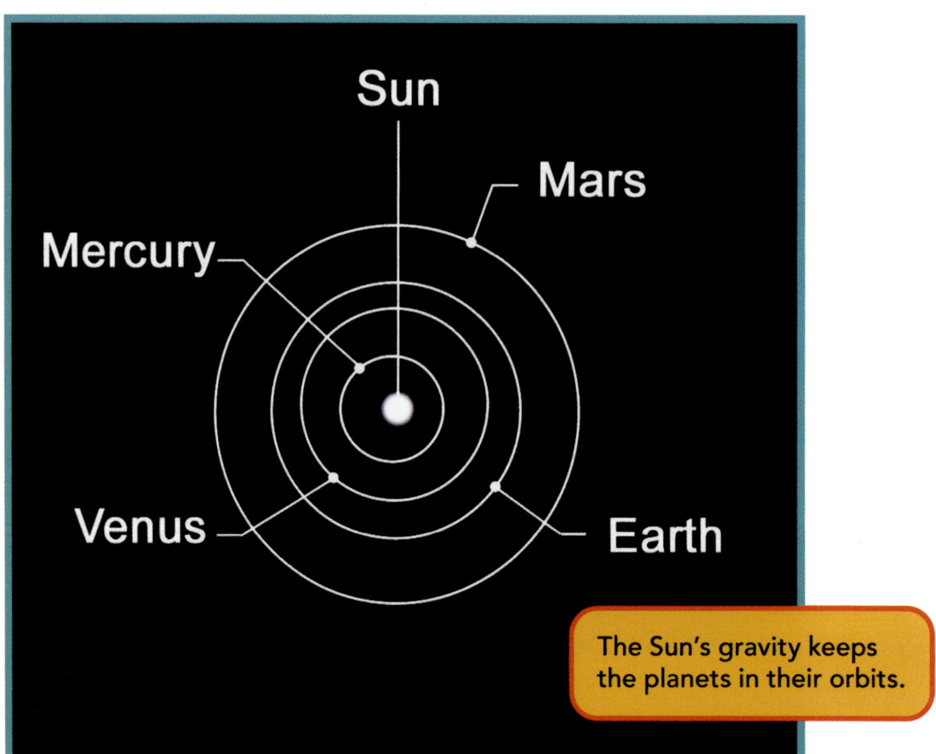

The Sun's gravity keeps the planets in their orbits.

Although the Sun can look big in our sky, it is very far from Earth.

Light travels faster than anything in the universe. But the Sun is far away from Earth. It takes eight minutes for the Sun's light to reach Earth.

Drive to the Sun

What if you could drive a car from Earth straight to the Sun? It would take about 170 years to get there!

The Sun is made of plasma. Hydrogen and helium make up most of the Sun.

The photosphere is the part of the Sun that we see. Sometimes it is called the Sun's surface. But it is not a solid surface you could stand on or a spacecraft could land on.

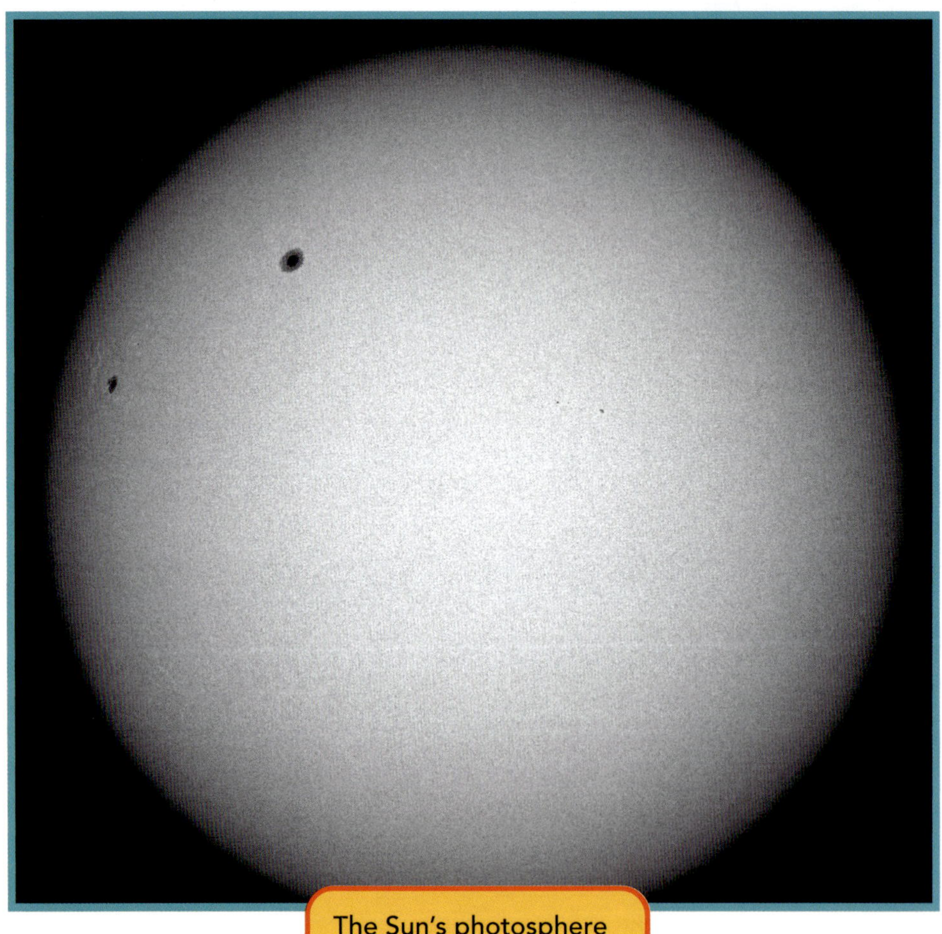

The Sun's photosphere

The inner layers of the Sun

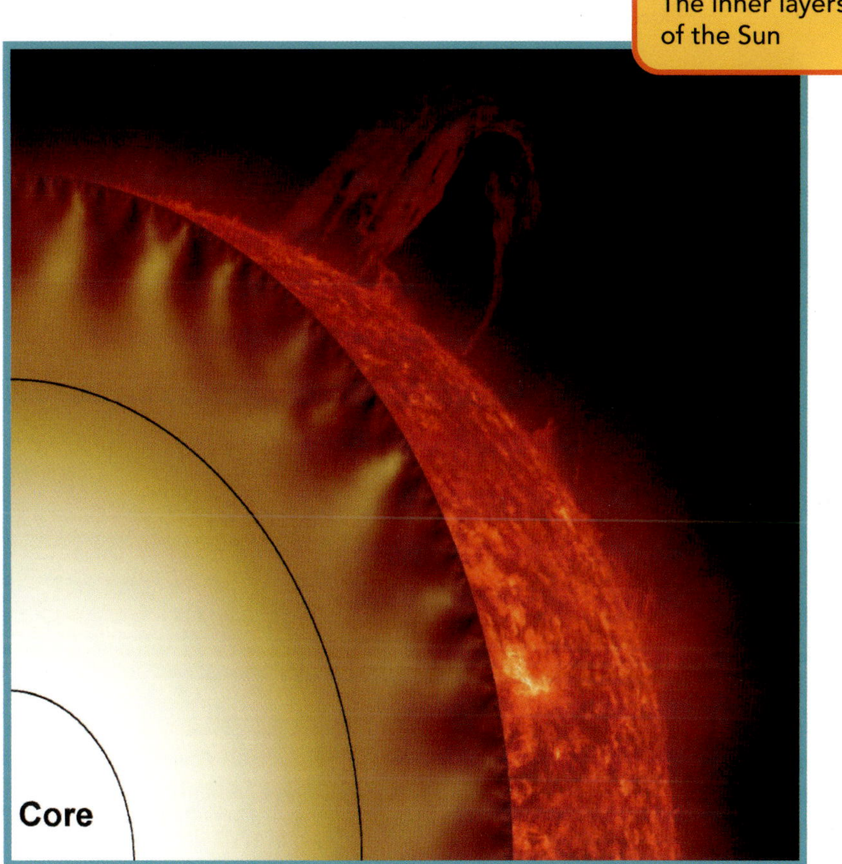

The Sun is very hot. The photosphere is about 9,000°F (5,000°C). That is much hotter than an oven or a fire.

The Sun's heat is made in its center. It's called the core. The temperature gets hotter deeper in the Sun. The center is about 27,000,000°F (15,000,000°C)!

WARNING!

Never stare at the Sun. Looking at it can hurt your eyes.

The Sun and Life on Earth

The Sun is the only star close enough to Earth to give the heat and light needed for life. Plants use light from the Sun to grow. Animals eat those plants to get energy. Energy from the Sun drives our weather, winds, and ocean currents.

Trees and other plants use sunlight for energy.

Aurora as seen in Alaska

The Sun also sends us small particles that hit Earth's atmosphere and cause auroras. Auroras are light shows in the sky. They are also called the northern lights or southern lights. They happen most often near Earth's North and South Poles.

CHAPTER 2

THE CHANGING SUN

Stars look like small dots in the night sky. But the Sun looks like a big, bright circle in the sky. The Sun looks bigger and brighter than other stars because the Sun is much closer to us on Earth.

The Sun shining in the sky

The Sun in Color

In drawings and pictures, the Sun is often yellow or orange. But the Sun is actually white! Earth's air can make it look yellow, orange, or even red. Many pictures add color to the Sun.

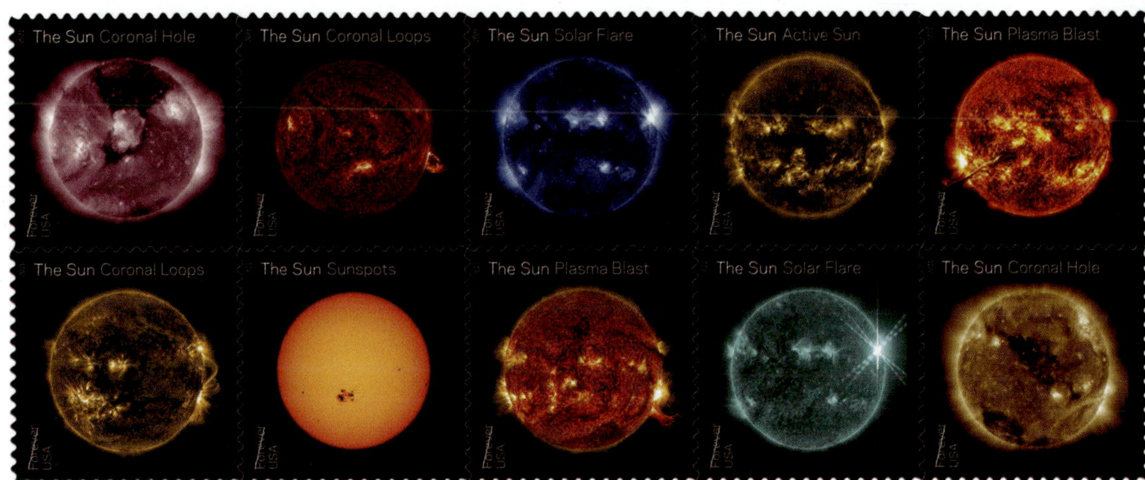

Images of the Sun taken by the Solar Dynamics Observatory (SDO) were used on stamps in 2021.

All stars are hot, but some are hotter than others. The color of a star depends on its temperature. The Sun and many other stars look white. Their light is a mix of the colors you see in a rainbow.

Stars hotter than the Sun look blue. Stars cooler than the Sun look red. So you may see stars in the night sky that look red, blue, or white.

Different colored stars as seen in this image of Orion and other constellations

A rainbow

When the Sun's white light hits water drops in Earth's air, the light bends. The light splits into different colors to make a rainbow. All the colors of the rainbow put together make the white color of the Sun.

UV Light and Sunspots

There are colors that we cannot see beyond the edges of a rainbow. One type is ultraviolet, or UV, light.

Some colors of UV light from the Sun get through Earth's atmosphere. It causes people to get suntans and sunburns. Other colors of UV light from the Sun get blocked by the atmosphere.

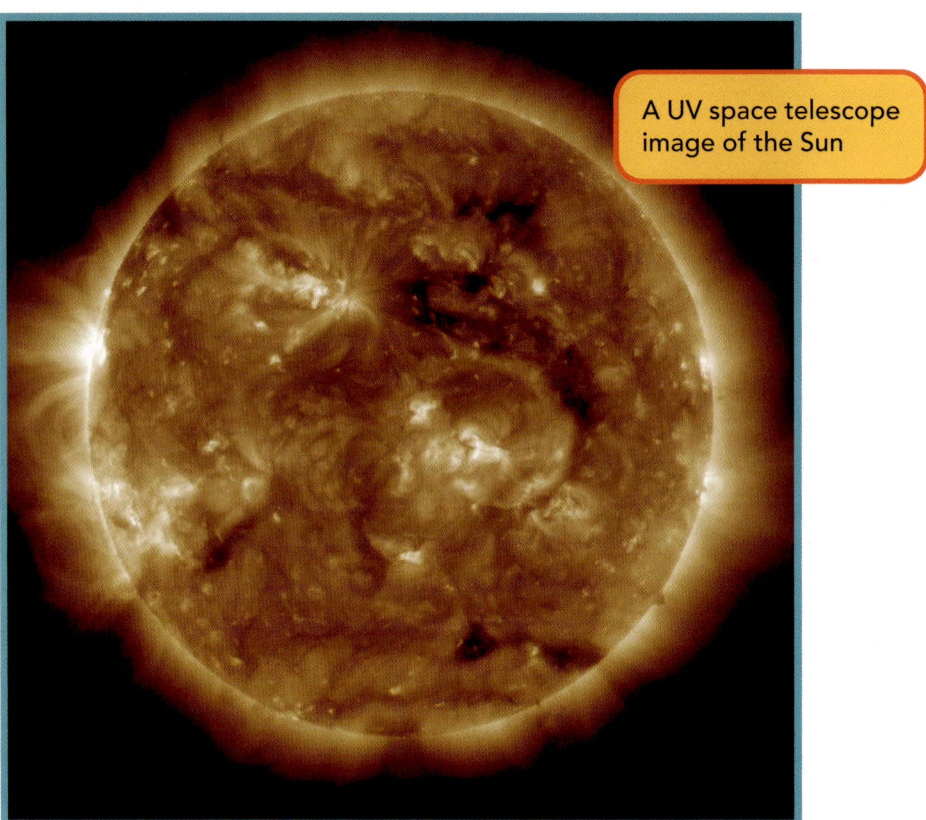

A UV space telescope image of the Sun

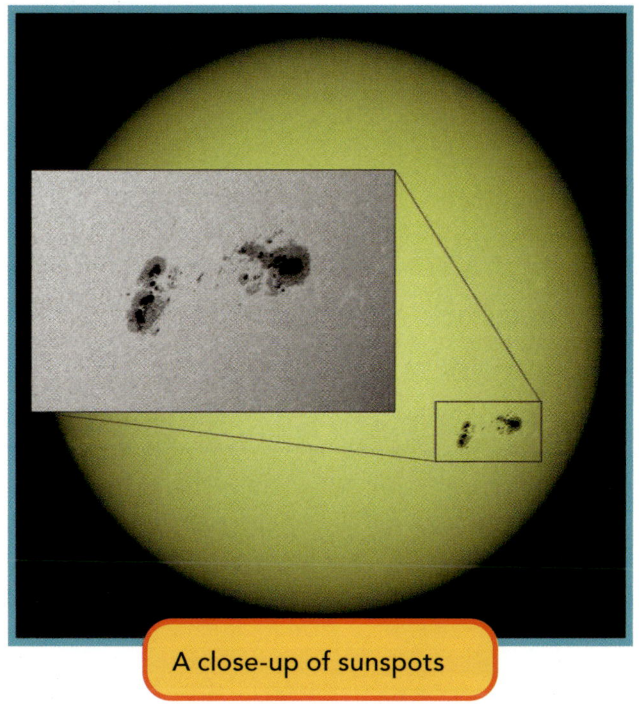

A close-up of sunspots

Some spacecraft that are above Earth's atmosphere have telescopes. Scientists use some of these space telescopes to see UV light and more details of the Sun. Many pictures of the Sun are UV pictures taken by space telescopes.

Sometimes the Sun has dark spots on it called sunspots. They are cooler than the area around them, so they look dark. Sunspots are caused by changes in the Sun's magnetic field. That is the area around a magnet where there is a magnetic force.

WARNING!

Never look directly at a solar eclipse. It's dangerous for your vision. Wear special eclipse glasses.

Solar Eclipses

A solar eclipse happens when the Moon passes between Earth and the Sun. This causes Earth to enter the Moon's shadow. The Moon blocks out the Sun.

A total solar eclipse happens when the Moon completely blocks the Sun. The corona, the Sun's thin outer atmosphere that is usually not visible, is visible. The Moon completely covers the Sun for about one to six minutes.

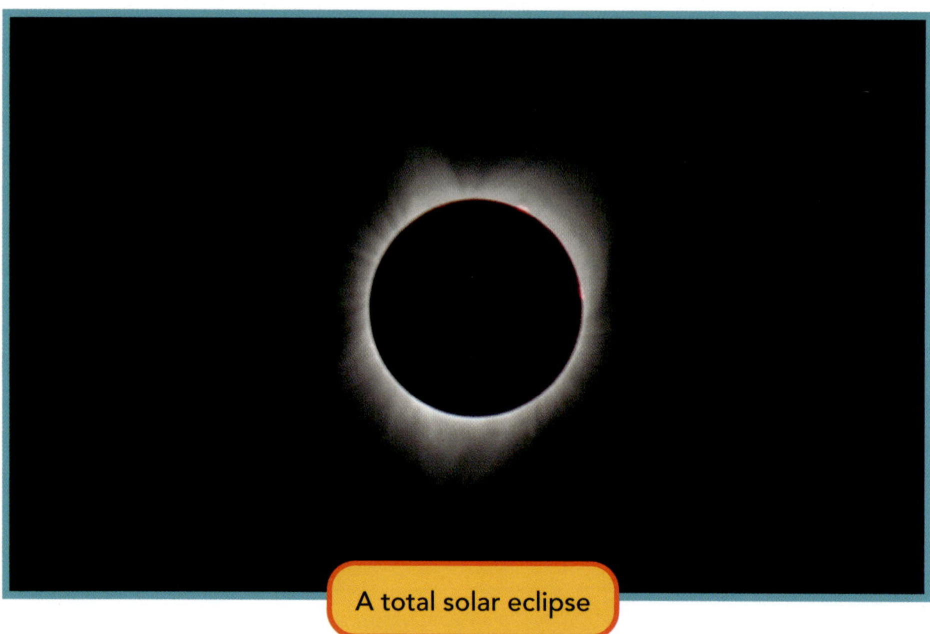

A total solar eclipse

Other Solar Eclipses

Solar eclipses sometimes only block part of the Sun. This happens during a partial solar eclipse. A ring of the Sun is left around the Moon in an annular solar eclipse.

A partial solar eclipse as seen with sunspots

CHAPTER 3

EXPLORING THE SUN

More than thirty robotic spacecraft have been launched to study the Sun. Spacecraft cannot land on the Sun since the Sun has no surface. And spacecraft cannot get close to the Sun because the Sun is so hot. But spacecraft have taught us much of what we know about the Sun.

An artwork of the SDO studying the Sun from Earth's orbit

Solar Missions

Some spacecraft point special solar telescopes at the Sun. They are able to see some colors of light that do not get through our atmosphere to the ground. That includes some UV light.

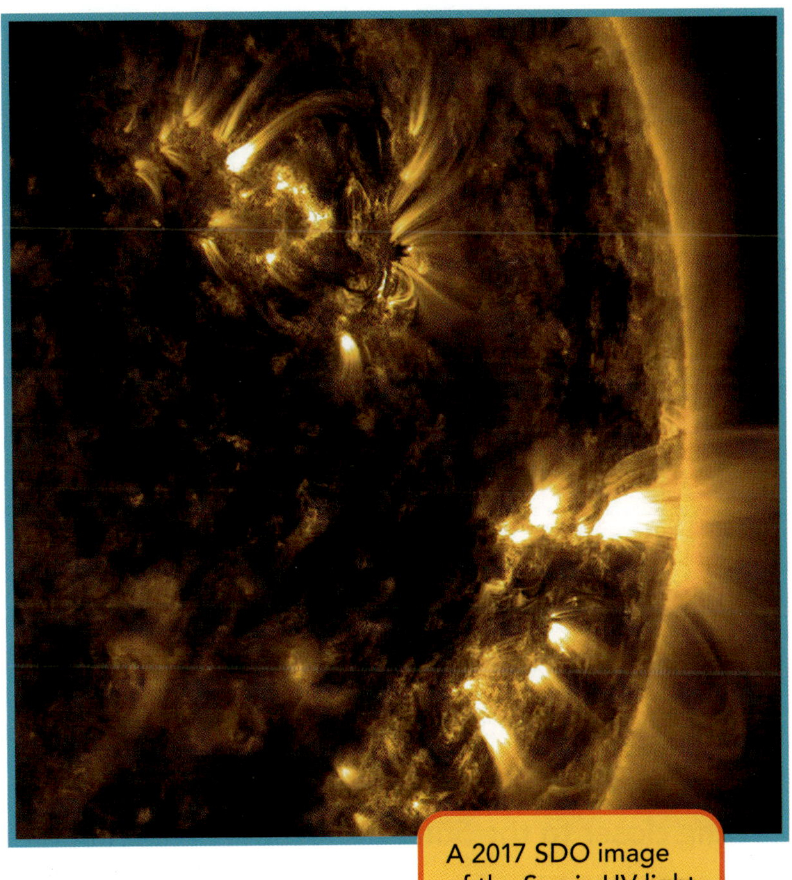

A 2017 SDO image of the Sun in UV light

The Parker Solar Probe has a special white heat shield at its top.

Building and flying spacecraft near the Sun is hard because of the Sun's extreme heat. The spacecraft that have tried getting closer to the Sun have often used heat shields. Heat shields point at the Sun to protect the rest of the spacecraft.

The Parker Solar Probe launched in 2018. It has flown about 4 million miles (6.4 million km) from the Sun. That is six times closer to the Sun than any other human-made object has flown. It has even flown through the Sun's upper atmosphere.

The Parker Solar Probe is also the fastest human-made object. It reaches 430,000 miles (692,000 km) per hour. That is fast enough to travel from Los Angeles to New York City in about twenty seconds.

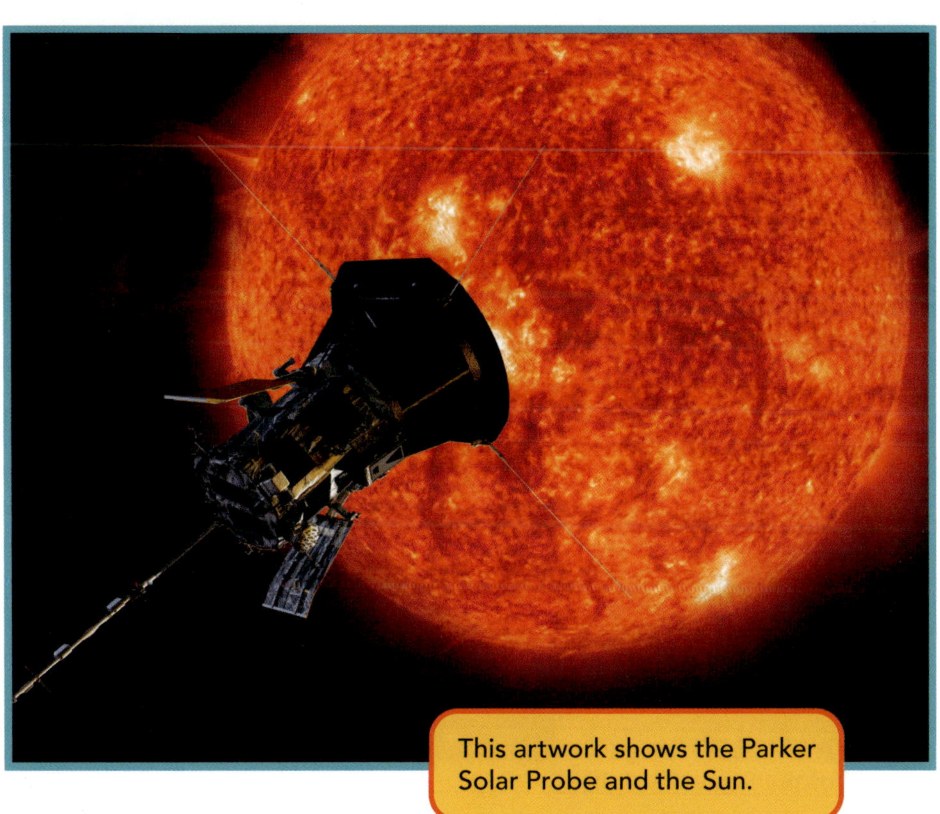

This artwork shows the Parker Solar Probe and the Sun.

An Important Star

The Sun is very important to our lives. The more we learn about the Sun, the more we learn about stars and the history of the solar system. We also learn more about how the Sun affects our lives now and how it will affect us in the future.

A 2018 SDO image of the Sun in UV light

A United Launch Alliance Delta IV Heavy rocket launches while carrying the Parker Solar Probe in 2018.

Glossary

atmosphere: the gases surrounding a planet, moon, or other body

gas: a state of matter with no fixed shape or volume

magnetic field: an area around a magnet where there is a magnetic force

mass: the total amount of matter that makes up an object

planet: a big, round, ball-shaped object that only goes around the Sun. Our solar system has eight planets. A planet does not have anything close to the same size near its orbit.

plasma: a state of matter that is like a gas with an electric charge

sunspot: dark spots that are cooler and darker than their surroundings and come and go on the Sun

ultraviolet (UV) light: light that your eyes cannot see and that has shorter wavelengths than visible light

Learn More

Betts, Bruce, PhD. *Casting Shadows: Solar and Lunar Eclipses with The Planetary Society ®*. Minneapolis: Lerner Publications, 2024.

Britannica Kids: Sun
https://kids.britannica.com/kids/article/Sun/353824

NASA Space Place: All about the Sun
https://spaceplace.nasa.gov/all-about-the-sun/en/

The Planetary Society: The Sun, Our Solar System's Star
https://www.planetary.org/worlds/the-sun

Schuh, Mari C. *The Sun: The Center of Our Solar System*. Minneapolis: Jump!, 2023.

Stratton, Connor. *The Sun*. Lake Elmo, MN: Focus Readers, 2023.

Index

Photo Acknowledgments

Image credits: F. Scott Schafer/The Planetary Society, p. 2; NASA/SDO, p. 4; NASA, pp. 6, 13; NASA/JPL, p. 7; NASA/JPL-Caltech/R. Hurt (SSC/Caltech), p. 8; SOHO (ESA & NASA), p. 9; NASA/Lunar and Planetary Institute, p. 10; Bruce Betts, pp. 11, 14, 16, 19, 22–23; NASA's Scientific Visualization Studio, p. 12; US Air Force/Senior Airman Joshua Strang, p. 15; NASA/U.S. Postal Service, p. 17; Wikimedia Commons (CC), p. 18; NASA/Wikimedia Commons (PD), pp. 24, 29; NASA/SDO/AIA, p. 20; NASA/GSFC/Solar Dynamics Observatory, pp. 21, 25, 28; NASA/Johns Hopkins APL/Lee Hobson, p. 26; NASA/Johns Hopkins APL/Steve Gribben, p. 27.
Cover: NASA/GSFC.

For my sons, Kevin and Daniel, and for all the members of The Planetary Society®

Lerner Publications Company
An imprint of Lerner Publishing Group, Inc.
241 First Avenue North
Minneapolis, MN 55401 USA

For reading levels and more information, look up this title at www.lernerbooks.com.

Main body text set in Aptifer Sans LT Pro. Typeface provided by Linotype AG.

Editor: Brianna Kaiser **Designer:** Mary Ross

Library of Congress Cataloging-in-Publication Data

Names: Betts, Bruce (PhD), author.
Title: The Sun : our solar system's star / Bruce Betts, PhD.
Description: Minneapolis, MN : Lerner Publications, [2025] | Series: Exploring our solar system with the Planetary Society | Includes bibliographical references and index. | Audience: Ages 7–10 | Audience: Grades 2–3 | Summary: "The Sun provides light and heat needed for life on Earth. Readers explore what the Sun is made of and how big it is, what we have learned about the Sun from spacecraft, and more"— Provided by publisher.
Identifiers: LCCN 2024009048 (print) | LCCN 2024009049 (ebook) | ISBN 9798765648285 (library binding) | ISBN 9798765661765 (paperback) | ISBN 9798765654712 (epub)
Subjects: LCSH: Sun—Juvenile literature
Classification: LCC QB521.5 .B485 2025 (print) | LCC QB521.5 (ebook) | DDC 523.7—dc23/eng/20240509

LC record available at https://lccn.loc.gov/2024009048
LC ebook record available at https://lccn.loc.gov/2024009049

Manufactured in the United States of America
1-1011033-53386-6/6/2024